Nowhere to Arrive

SERIES EDITORS

Chris Abani

John Alba Cutler

Reginald Gibbons

Susannah Young-ah Gottlieb

Ed Roberson

Matthew Shenoda

Nowhere to Arrive

Poems

Jenny Xie

NORTHWESTERN UNIVERSITY PRESS

EVANSTON, ILLINOIS

Northwestern University Press
www.nupress.northwestern.edu

Northwestern University Poetry and Poetics Colloquium
poetry.northwestern.edu

Printed in the United States of America

10   9   8   7   6   5   4   3   2   1

Library of Congress Cataloging-in-Publication Data
Names: Xie, Jenny, author.
Title: Nowhere to arrive : poems / Jenny Xie.
Other titles: Drinking gourd chapbook poetry prize.
Description: Evanston, Illinois : Northwestern University Press, 2017. |
Series: The drinking gourd chapbook poetry prize
Identifiers: LCCN 2016044877 | ISBN 9780810135086 (pbk. : alk. paper)
Subjects: LCSH: Travel—Poetry.
Classification: LCC PS3624.I4 .N69 2017 | DDC 811.3—dc23
LC record available at https://lccn.loc.gov/2016044877

First there is a mountain.
Then there is no mountain.
Then there is.

Contents

Foreword

Chris Abani

In *Nowhere to Arrive*, Jenny Xie begins the search for home, roots, and herself certain that these things cannot be found. The idea is that the deeper truth of the quest lies not in what is found or arrived at, but rather in the shape and texture of the search; it is a clever conceit paralleled in Homi Bhabha's ideas about identity, which he refers to as a state of flux rather than a destination. In the hands of a less accomplished poet, this could go very wrong, but when the opening poem, "Rootless," ends with a couplet like this one, you know you're in adept hands:

> Now, on this sleeper train, there's nowhere to arrive.
> Me, I'm just here in my traveller's clothes, trying on each passing
> town for size.

The chapbook moves quickly from here through the movements of the quest—"Phnom Penh Diptych: Wet Season" and "Phnom Penh Diptych: Dry Season," through "Corfu"—to the last poem, "Ongoing," which is a mirror for the opening "Rootless," with the deft sureness of a symphonic composition. The movements are lush and sensuous:

> It's useless to describe this slurry of humidity or the joy of a fistful
> of rice creating curry, but it is not that I have a loss for words.

It is also a self-critical examination devoid of self-indulgence:

> Every day I drink Coca-Cola and write ad copy.
> I'm in the business of multiplying needs.

What is understood here is deeper than the existential, something that Lacan delves into when he explores the gestalt of desire and its insatiability:

Desire makes beggars out of each and every one of us.

Xie's journey is full of this complex calculus of loss and gain, movement and inertia, joy and ennui. The language of this book is delightfully rich and spare at the same time, and the poet's sense of the line reveals confidence. So much is brought to rest on the most quiet moments. In "Displacement," the poet confronts us with the true struggle of the artist and thus of this book, with the understanding that the very moment of epiphany, of artistic ecstasy, is also the moment of estrangement. In other words, each revelation moves the quest deeper to another desire, an endless peeling onion of self.

When Xie arrives in the poem "Ongoing," the reader too has arrived, not at any specific place but rather at the acceptance that there is no clear destination. It is a hard-won grace in this acceptance of purpose over outcome, of the shaping of questions:

She had trained herself to look for answers at eye level
but they were lower, they were changing all the time.

Without ever taking the easy way out, this poet has crafted a book of questions and a book of sensual search. It is a beautiful one and we will all be enriched for reading it.

Rootless

Between Hanoi and Sapa there are paunched hills
and no two brick houses in a row.

I mean, no *three*—
Counting's hard in half-sleep, and the rain pulls a sheet

over the sugar palms and their waxed leaves.
Hours ago, I spotted a motorbike with a hog strapped to its back,

the size of a date pit from the distance.
The mind wonders if the two are the same:

rootless and unhooked from the ground, like seasons.
No matter. My frugal mouth spends the only foreign words it owns.

Now, on this sleeper train, there's nowhere to arrive.
Me, I'm just here in my traveler's clothes, trying on each passing town
     for size.

Phnom Penh Diptych: Wet Season

August, chambered. City of a million young faces.

A woman perches sidesaddle on a motorbike.
Another clutches stiff bread and leeks.

And how combed through, this rain!

The riled heat reaches the river shoal before it reaches the dark.

•

New money laps at these streets.
Indecipherable thirsts planted beneath high-rises.

Norodom Avenue, flanked by watery bulbs,
lets through a motorcade.

In the backseat of a gold Lexus
a minister's son lies, his eyes shut
dumb with honeyed sleep.

•

Fixtures: suitcases with their lips slack, lukewarm showers up to three times in a day.

Mosquito bites on the arms and thighs, patterned like pips on dice.

An hour before midnight, the corners of the city begin to peel.
Alley of sex workers, tinny folk songs pushed through speakers.
Fluorescent karaoke bars bracketed by vendors hawking salted crickets.

How do the eyes and ears keep pace?

•

The zippered notes of bike engines enter
through an opening in my sleep.

My dreams sputtering out because of this.

•

It's useless to describe the slurry of humidity or the joy of a fistful of rice cradled in curry, but it's not that I'm at a loss for words.

Every day I drink Coca-Cola and write ad copy.
I'm in the business of multiplying needs.

Today, it's whitening face lotion, whitening foam wash, whitening
    sunscreen.
Across the seas, the copy can only read *brightening*.

But here, things blanch.

•

Desire makes beggars out of each and every one of us.

A cavity that cannot close.
That cracks open more distances.

A man whose outline I know dives into a rooftop pool,
rips a body-sized hole into it.

Wanting falls around me. Heavy garment.

•

After clocking out, a group of telecom managers tear into durians.

And now that the day turns its back, new wives buckle limbs with foreign lovers at the Himawari Hotel.

Someone sweeps thick cockroaches from the floor, someone orders oysters on ice.

Even the rain sweats, unkempt like the rest of us.

•

I enter Wat Langka to sit.
To still the breath.
A steadying out and in, out and in.

Still, here in this country, something I can't ever enter.

•

On the screen: glow of missives.

Friends with pressed collars riding elevators.
They pass on left lanes, laboring in the din of American cities.

Shot nerves.

The stock market begins to show
imperceptible cracks.

•

The irony of the White Building is lost on no one.

It's a face repeatedly emptied by a fist.
It hangs on by dirtied rag, by pure stubbornness.

I've lived across from it, walked past neighbors
gambling on Nokia phones held together by elastic bands
and grandmothers fanning coals to smoke fish.

For my own apartment, I paid too much.
In the kitchen, I catch myself in a pan of water, but there I am
    transparent.

You could say moving all the way here was a kind of hiding.

•

The compass needle points to where nothing begins.

A line that cuts through
four towns and two international cities.

Yes, I'm tired of laundry soured by mildew,
this loneliness turning over
when it smells my approach.

•

Rainwater mars the tin roofs,
melts a sticky bun left in the alley.
It worries down the final tips of daylight.

How long will it be like this?

Water growing on water.

•

The tourists curate vacation stories,
their viewfinders slice into the horizon so cleanly—

Their shrill pleasure.

•

I wake up one morning to find beauty suspect.

Outside, a vendor hacks at a slab of ice
while two teenaged boys wait for crushed
sugar cane juice on matching motorbikes.

Commonplace nouns.

    A rain that chases
    the tail of my silence until sundown.

Phnom Penh Diptych: Dry Season

Motorbikes darting. Nattering horns leave their aftertaste.

I mark the distance on a map: this city a wrist-width away from the last.

The street dogs turn their thoughts to water, wet foods.

It's not easy to measure your life in debts.

•

For years now, I've been using the wrong palette.
Each year with its itchy blue, as the bruise of solitude reaches its
    expiration date.

Planes and buses, guesthouse to guesthouse.

I've gotten to where I am by dint of my poor eyesight,
my overreactive motion sickness.

9 P.M., Hanoi's Old Quarter: duck porridge and plum wine.

    Voices outside the door come to a soft boil.

•

The Australian down the hall tells me she sleeps naked every night
with a checkered krama scarf she's wet with water and refrigerated.

Then I turn the fan and fix it on me, it's the only way.

A little relief as she slides from an early hour
into a suffocating one.

.

My guilt goes off on a trip,
then returns, wilder.

All I do is recede from the view
of those at my back.

Heeding only the tug of the interior.

•

It's not about happiness, though I forget why I came.

Perhaps it's shallow sleep in the subtropics,
my youthful ambitions wet and slack.

I wring them out.

I want to remember this, though not with wistfulness.
I hang my expectations out on a string.

The city warms its tongue by not saying anything.

·

Wooden spirit houses on the road to Kampot spray-painted gold, capacious enough for a pot of incense, rice, and one can of Fanta.

Noon, white hour.

The outlines of bungalows in the distance—impossible to part the seen and unseen. What's here and what isn't.

The language behind this language cracks open like a sea crab.

●

Months of medium-rare insomnia.

    A pot of wine has me confuse
    elation with clarity, and so I traverse
    the night market, my purse empty.

The moon hardens on a hot skillet.

    All that is untouchable as far as the eye can see.

•

I thought I owned my worries, but here I was, pulled along by the
needle of genetics, by my mother's tendency to pry at openings in her life.

Calls made from a booth where one pays by the minute.

No, I haven't traveled here for the lawlessness.

I fail to mention the bite of my mistakes,
furnish stories with movement
and no shades of despair.

●

Beauty, too, can become oppressive if you let it,
but that's only if you stay long enough.

If you stay long enough,
the heat's fingers will touch everything
and the imprint will sting.

•

I kept twisting my face in bar bathrooms,
in wet markets, in strangers' arms.
And the years here—
they rolled past,
one by one, in a line.

•

Men and women came and went.
The city was dry, and then it wasn't.

I lost track of the time.

Corfu

To the north and to the west: dark tips of cypress. Corfu in the slow
math of July, and this reservoir of fear running low. The island has two
hard-boiled hills—the bus descends one of them, blaring folk ballads.
Houses the color of custard, some burnt. A Greek Orthodox monastery
where even female cats can't enter. I've never set foot on this island
before, but all day a familiar version of this self insists like a plain sweat
stain against my back.

Pickpocketed days ago in France, all my dollars and euros gone.
Yesterday, I landed in an airport so small I could see from one end to the
other.

I've grown lean from only eating the past.

One line through customs,
and the plane impossibly close to the sea.
No ceremony in any of it.

Displacement

The woman by the soap stand with the low neckline is beside herself.
Ecstasy, from the Greek *ekstasis*, meaning "to stand outside oneself."
Estranged. In Kerkyra, beneath chalky sun, I put down coins for ice
coffee and a shot of kumquat liquor. Her crying jags force me into
attention.

Pain displaces. Joy to be sloughed, stranger to oneself. These patterns of
movement are ancient. This morning, the boat guide told us that long
before the debt crisis, fishermen on the island fled into the watery caves
to escape their wives.

Crumbled rust on boat metal.
In order to dock the boat,
the fisherman throws all his weight against the line.

Fortified

The Old Fortress in Corfu Town rests on a promontory, with Albania's mountains legible to the east. In the sixteenth century, the Venetians dug a moat around it to protect it from the Turks. Today there's no sign of disorder, just the white sailboats of the rich moored in the quay like grains of rice. No one here knows me, which swells my appetite for this island tenfold. Climb alone to the top to look down on pit-colored roofed verandas, the olive and the scrub. Lunch of sour yogurt thickened with cucumber.

On the bus ride back,
we pass a store named Ni Hao, selling pelts.
Hello in all directions.

Epistle

Eavesdropping on a mother
needling at her mule-brained son

stopping by the side of the road
to examine the dry socket of Agios Georgios

the face of this year's summer is long
all those years I was spared of seeing myself through myself

now the days clear like a yawn
distance giving autonomy the arid space to grow

I'll rinse later this afternoon in the sea
then compose lines to you of reasonable length

to say the opening you left is wide enough for me
but I'm stunned to love this aloneness

Ongoing

Never mind the distances traveled, the companion
she made of herself. The threadbare twenties not
to be underestimated. A wild depression that burned
January through April. And still, some part of her pecks away.
Relationships annealed through shared grievances.
The pages that steadied her. Books prowled her
until the hard daybreak, and for months after.
Separating new vows from the old, like laundry whites.
Tangles along the way the comb-teeth
of the mind had to bite through, but for what.
She had trained herself to look for answers at eye level,
but they were lower, they were changing all the time.

Acknowledgments

I am indebted to Chris Abani, John Alba Cutler, Reginald Gibbons, Susannah Young-ah Gottlieb, Ed Roberson, and Matthew Shenoda at the Northwestern University Poetry and Poetics Colloquium for making this chapbook possible.

Additional thanks to the editors of *Oxford Poetry Review* and *cream city review*, where several of these poems, some in previous versions, originally appeared.

I am deeply grateful for my friends, teachers, and the following organizations and institutions for their invaluable support and community: the English and creative writing departments at Princeton University, the NYU Creative Writing Program, Kundiman, the Elizabeth George Foundation, the Fine Arts Work Center in Provincetown, Poets and Writers, the Cave Canem Foundation's Writing Across Cultures workshops, and Brooklyn Zen Center.

Jenny Xie's work appears in *Tin House*, *The New Republic*, *Harvard Review*, *The Literary Review*, *Los Angeles Review of Books*, and elsewhere. She teaches at New York University and lives in Brooklyn.